Angels To The Rescue

A Story of Change, Helplessness and Rescue

Lawrence Balleine

Parson's Porch Books

Angels To The Rescue: A Story of Change, Helplessness and Rescue

ISBN: Softcover 978-1-955581-19-6

Copyright © 2021 by Lawrence Balleine

All rights reserved. No part of this book may be reproduced or transmitted in any form or by any means, electronic or mechanical, including photocopying, recording, or by any information storage and retrieval system, without permission in writing from the publisher.

Parson's Porch Books is an imprint of Parson's Porch & Company (PP&C) in Cleveland, Tennessee. PP&C is an innovative organization which raises money by publishing books of noted authors, representing all genres. Its face and voice is **David Russell Tullock** (dtullock@parsonsporch.com).

Parson's Porch & Company *turns books into bread & milk* by sharing its profits with the poor.

www.parsonsporch.com

Angels To The Rescue
A Story of Change, Helplessness and Rescue

Introduction

ANGELS TO THE RESCUE is the fifth and final segment of a series that traces the sabbatical travel of Michael Lattimore. As in the previous volumes, Michael, the chief character in each of the books, continues his journey to the dairy farming regions of Wisconsin. A middle school social studies teacher, he is seeking to determine how the changes in culture are affecting the family farm. Along the way, he meets numerous people facing a variety of circumstances. These lead Michael into interactions that he never could have foreseen prior to his departure. Whereas ENTERTAINING ANGELS is a story of change, loss and healing, AN ANGEL AMONG US focuses on change, brokenness and reconciliation, ANGELS IN DISGUISE examines change, loss, and new beginnings, and ENCOURAGING ANGELS explores change, fear and encouragement, ANGELS TO THE RESCUE centers on change, helplessness, and rescue.

Friday Morning

The free breakfast at the Sky View Inn was bare bones: coffee, juice, and donuts. Yet it was enough to fill the void in Michael's stomach and sustain him for at least a couple of hours. After he washed down his second donut with a glass of apple juice, he checked out of the motel and made his way to Rib Mountain State Park.

Upon entering the park, Michael sensed that he had been there before. And he had been. When he was five years old, his family had visited this scenic location. He had not been back since. As he drove up the winding road to the top of the mountain, Michael flashed back to that first visit. He had a vivid memory of looking down from the mountain's summit to the farmland below. The view was awesome. Obviously, his one and only previous visit to Rib Mountain had made a lasting impression.

As he continued his ascent, he recalled that Wisconsin had a couple of higher "hills" that reached altitudes slightly greater than that of Rib Mountain. He considered Timm's Hill, located about an hour northwest of Rib Mountain, which extends 1952 feet above sea level. Although Rib Mountain stands ten feet shorter, it has always been considered a mountain. It's probably because at 1942 feet above sea level, Rib Mountain stretches 741 feet above the surrounding terrain. No other mountain or hill in Wisconsin boasts a greater difference in height from its peak to the surrounding terrain.

When Michael reached the summit, he parked his

pickup and walked to the overlook.

He soon arrived at the location that offered a panoramic view that extended for miles. Michael immediately knew he was standing at the very same spot that he had stood as a five-year-old. But what he saw now was not as he remembered it. Yes there were still plenty of farms with their red barns and fields sporting a variety of crops, but much of what spread out below him was now urban sprawl – homes, businesses, schools, and parks. Wausau, the city at the base of the mountain, had certainly grown.

Michael mumbled: "Another change to rural life. I wonder how urban expansion has affected those dairy farmers whose land is now longer being used for crops or pasture."

Michael decided to sit on a nearby bench as he gazed to the north. He soon found himself recalling a visit to another mountain that he and Elaine, and their two children – Sarah and Simon – had made several years earlier. They had left their Midwestern home on the day after Sarah had been confirmed. Their initial destination was Cape Cod, a peninsula that extends into the Atlantic Ocean from the eastern edge of Massachusetts. After a week's stay on the Cape, their route home included a stop at Mount Monadnock in southern New Hampshire. Finding a hiking trail leading to its summit, the Lattimore family began their ascent. With its peak at 3165 feet above sea level, Mount Monadnock is certainly not the highest mountain in the Appalachian chain. Nevertheless, the trail to the top of the mountain offered a significant challenge.

After hiking for nearly an hour and a half, they reached the summit. Michael suddenly realized why mountains play such a dominant role in both the Hebrew scriptures and the New Testament. For standing at the top of Mount Monadnock, he felt close to God – both physically and emotionally. He even said to Sarah: "Up here, there seems to be nothing separating us from the heavens. Doesn't it make you feel close to God?"

Sarah agreed.

It was an exhilarating experience as Michael considered Moses who received the Law on Mount Sinai, the prophet Jeremiah who challenged the prophets of Baal on Mount Carmel, and Abraham who ascended the mountain with his son Isaac. And then there was Jesus and his famous "Sermon on the Mount" and his transfiguration on yet another mountain. Mountains, Michael realized, were the locations of significant interactions between God and humanity. "No wonder," he said to Sarah, "a person feels close to God when they ascend mountains." And then he said to himself: I wouldn't be surprised if a lot of pastors have offered their congregations a series of sermons based on Biblical stories whose settings are mountains.

Michael's thoughts returned to the present. He was now on the tenth day of a sabbatical journey that was taking him to several of the dairy farming regions of Wisconsin. A middle school social studies teacher from Green Bay, he had received a grant to study how the changes of the past thirty years were a affecting dairy farmers and their families.

The biggest change he noted was that the number of

dairy farms had decreased dramatically. He knew that when he was in high school, Wisconsin had nearly 90,000 active dairy farms; now less than 10,000 remained. And the trend continued. Over the past ten days, Michael noted that whenever he picked up a local newspaper, it included advertisements for farm auctions. Often occupying nearly half a page, these notices indicated the land, machinery and cattle that were to be sold. Michael also came to realize that although the number of farms and herds continued to plummet, the number of dairy cows had remained fairly constant. Thus, Wisconsin's cows continued to produce 15% of the nation's milk, 25% of its butter, and 30% of its cheese.

A hawk soared overhead, momentarily capturing Michael's attention. After the raptor descended out of sight, Michael thought: If I want to be home by tonight, I better get on my way. Even though I allowed for two weeks on the road, ten full days is long enough. I think that I've gathered enough information to fulfill my quest. And, after learning of Ali's pregnancy on Wednesday, I'm anxious to get home.

As he stood, Michael felt renewed and energized. He wondered if it was that way for the early disciples – Peter, James, and John -- who had accompanied Jesus up the mountain where Jesus was transfigured. In that experience, Jesus' appearance had been altered and his clothes became dazzling white. These three followers saw Jesus in a new way – transfigured -- and that vision helped to strengthen them for the journey ahead. It was a journey that would take them to Jerusalem where Jesus would be arrested, persecuted, and crucified.

Michael returned to his pickup and began his descent. When he reached the base of the mountain he reviewed his planned route for the day. Again, as had been his practice for his entire journey, he would take back roads and lesser traveled highways as much as possible. Thus, he would travel east on Highway 29 for only a short distance before turning south onto County Highway J. Then he would pick up a lesser traveled state highway that would lead him further east.

Friday Later Morning

Shortly after turning onto County Highway J, Michael thought: Another change, as he admired a barn quilt that was fastened to the side of a large red barn located to his right.

Barn quilts are a fairly recent addition to the rural landscape. Although they are not made of fabric, they do resemble patchwork quilts. Constructed of large wood panels, they are painted in such a way as to produce unique "quilt-like" patterns or designs. Most are square-shaped, and measure about 8 feet by 8 feet. When they first appeared, Michael thought they would just be a passing fad. But they had grown in popularity and Michael had seen scores of them during the past week and half. He now figured that "they're here to stay." In fact, a week earlier as he passed through Green County, Michael had secured a visitor's guide to the county. It included an article that illustrated the barn quilts found in Green County. There were over one hundred and fifty and each had its own unique design.

Indeed, Michael noted that no two barn quilts he had seen on his road trip were alike in color or design. He wondered if each quilt had its own story to tell. He decided that next time he saw one he would stop and inquire about it. It didn't take him long. The next barn on the right sported a colorful quilt. Michael decided to pull in and just as he did, he saw a fella in tan Carhartt overalls approaching the side door of the barn. The man noticed Michael pull in his driveway. He turned from the door and headed toward Michael.

Michael stopped, rolled down his window and said: "Fine day."

The farmer responded: "Fine day indeed. Can I help you with anything?"

"I'm quite sure you can. I've been driving around the state for the past ten days. And I've been noticing the barn quilts. They're all different. Do the designs and colors carry any special meaning? Are they meant to tell some sort of story?"

"Well, I can't speak for anybody else, but I can tell you about ours."

Both Michael and the farmer turned their attention to the multi-colored quilt that continued to be visible from where Michael had parked.

"I'll start with the four squares at each of the corners. You see them? Two light blue and two pink ones – that's because we have four children – two boys and two girls. We appreciate the four seasons. That's why you see the rectangular shapes connecting those four squares. The light green one is for spring, the darker green represents summer, the orange is for autumn, and obviously, the white stands for winter."

The farmer continued: "We're Lutheran and we've always appreciated the seasons that comprise the church year."

Michael nodded his head causing the fella to say: "You seem to know what I'm talking about."

Michael replied: "I know exactly what you're talking about. I learned about the church year in confirmation class years ago."

"Then you probably know each season is designated by a color. For Advent and Lent the color is purple; the Easter and Christmas seasons are white; and Epiphany and the season of the Trinity are green. And Pentecost Day and Reformation Sunday are red. Well, you see that large multi-colored ring right in the middle of the quilt? We call it our 'liturgical color wheel.' The ring represents the church year. The biggest portion of it is green; that's because green is associated with the season of the Trinity, and that season is the longest – usually about half a year. The smaller green section of the ring represents the Epiphany season. You might remember it goes from January 6th to the start of Lent. The two sections of white are for the Christmas and Easter seasons, and the purple is for Advent and Lent. And do you see the little slashes of red?

"Pentecost Day and Reformation Sunday," Michael interjected.

"Precisely. You sure do remember the liturgical colors."

"That's one confirmation lesson that has stuck with me."

The man continued: "Instead of a cross in the middle of the circle, we've placed a fish. You probably know that a fish was a very early symbol for Christianity."

"Interesting," commented Michael. "What about all the blue and yellow that is filling in all the left-over space?" Michael asked.

"Well, with a name like Olson, my ancestors came from Sweden; and those are the colors on the flag of Sweden."

"Fascinating," said Michael. "I've been seeing all kinds of barn quilts the last week and a half. I bet many of them have a story to tell."

"I would think that many do. Rosie and I realize that our quilt probably has little meaning for anybody but us. But we know what it means to us. And I suppose that's all that matters."

"Well, now I too know what it means. And I appreciate you sharing its story with me. By the way, my name is Michael – Michael Lattimore."

"Well, I hate to run off, Michael, but I've got an ailing calf and I've got to check on her. Actually, I thought you may have been the vet."

"No problem. Thank you for taking time to speak with me, Mr. Olson."

"Robert's my first name. I'm glad you stopped by."

Michael reached out and shook Robert's hand.

As Robert returned to the barn to attend to his calf, Michael turned around in the Olson's wide gravel driveway. When Michael reached the end of the driveway, he stopped for a pickup truck that was approaching from the left. The truck slowed and pulled in the driveway. Both the pickup driver and Michael waved to each other. As the pickup passed alongside of Michael's vehicle, Michael read the words on the door panel: "MID-STATE VETERINARY SERVICE."

Throughout his travels Michael had come to appreciate Wisconsin's rich and diverse ethnic heritage. He remembered reading several publications from the Wisconsin Ethnic Settlement Trail which identified the ethnicity of many communities along the Lake Michigan shoreline. He knew that Manitowoc County – the place of his childhood and youth – had been largely settled by Czechs and Poles. In fact, he recalled that as a child he would often hear older folks speaking in their "native tongue." And those who did speak English often carried an accent that they said was a carry-over from "the old country." By that, they meant either Czechoslovakia or Poland.

Many other areas near the Lake Michigan shoreline had been settled by various groups from Germany. Additionally, Cedar Grove and Oostburg were Dutch. Door County's earlier settlers came from Sweden and Norway. And interestingly, Washington Island, located off the northern tip of the Door County Peninsula was settled by folks from Iceland. Michael noted how many of these ethnic groups settled in the areas where the terrain resembled their homeland.

After remaining in close proximity to Lake Michigan for his first day and a half of travel, Michael had turned west – away from the Lake. He quickly noticed that many of the ethnic groups found along the Lake Michigan shoreline had also established settlements inland. Knowing that Wisconsin was largely settled in the mid to late 1800's by immigrants from a variety of European countries, Michael noted how these "newcomers" – when they constructed their barns – often copied the style of barns from their place of origin. So as he traveled, he had begun to tell the difference between a Norwegian barn and a Swiss one; a German structure and one built by Belgians. And then Michael reminded himself that prior to being settled by European immigrants, what is now Wisconsin was home to several Native American groups including: Menominee, Ho Chunk, Ojibwe, Potawatomi, and others.

Michael had also been paying attention to silos. Many were concrete stave, some were metal, and a few were constructed using field stones. He had also seen two wood stave silos. The wooden ones would have been the earliest to have been built. Michael would often guess the age of a farm by the style of its silo or set of silos.

Then he remembered that dairy farms were not the first farms in Wisconsin. Rather, Wisconsin's earliest farms raised wheat. In 1860, Wisconsin had been the nation's second largest producer of wheat. But by the 1870's, wheat production was on the decline and dairy farming gained a strong foothold.

Michael had driven about five miles beyond the Olson farm when instead of a barn quilt, he saw the year 1905 displayed on a large red barn. Above the four numbers was the name "Duffy." Another century old farm,

Michael thought. During the past ten days, he had observed several barns that indicated the year in which the farm was established. The oldest he had seen was located in southwestern Dane County. It had been established in 1855. Michael wondered if this had always been a dairy farm, or if began as a wheat farm.

About a half mile after passing the Duffy barn, he came to the intersection of County Highways J and Q. He considered turning left onto Q, but he realized it would take him back to State Highway 29, and he wanted to avoid highly traveled highways. Yet he felt compelled to turn onto Q. And if there was one thing Michael had learned during his days of travel, it was to trust his instincts. So he "went with his gut" and turned onto Q.

A moment later he came over a rise and saw two figures walking along the side of the road. They were about one hundred yards ahead of them. As he slowed he got a closer look at them. One was a small child about four or five years old and the other appeared to be an older gentleman. Grandpa and grandchild out for a morning walk on a nice clear day, assumed Michael.

Michael slowed to about twenty miles per hour and waved as he passed them. But neither the child nor man waved back. That's strange, thought Michael, folks in the country always wave. About a half mile down the road Michael felt he needed to turn around and check on them.

As he draw within fifty feet of the pair, Michael noticed the little child – a girl wearing shorts and a T shirt with Mickey Mouse printed on the front --

appeared to be crying. "That's really strange. Something's not right," Michael blurted out. Michael recalled his outings as a young child with his own grandpa and they were always happy times. "Something must be wrong." Michael pulled over to the side of the road, got out of his pickup and approached the two.

"Who are you and what do you want?" snapped the gentleman in bib overalls. He appeared to be in his late 60's or early 70's.

"I'm Michael and I stopped to see if everything is OK with you."

"Of course it is. I'm with my daughter Mary Ann and we're out for a nice walk."

Michael thought it was strange that the man called the little girl his daughter. It seemed unlikely he would have such a young daughter. His suspicions were immediately confirmed when the little girl, who had ceased her sobbing, spoke: "Grandpa, my name isn't Mary Ann. That's mommy's name. I'm Claire and you're Grandpa."

"Oh, I forgot," said the gentleman.

"Where are you off to?" asked Michael.

"None of your business," came the terse reply from the man.

Then the girl said, "I just wanted to go with grandpa for a walk, and now, we don't know how to get home."

Kneeling down in front of the young child, Michael asked: "You said your name is Claire. Do you know your full name?"

"It's the name of a bird. Robin something."

"Robinson?" Michael guessed.

"Yes, that's it," Claire replied. "I'm Claire Robinson."

Michael thought that their home must not be too far away. And then he noticed it. Stitched on Claire's grandpa's cap were the words: "Duffy Farms." The name on the barn about a half mile back on the other road was Duffy. I bet that's their home or maybe the home of some of their relatives, reasoned Michael.

Michael said: "I think I can get you home. You're welcome to hop in my pickup truck and I'll take you there."

"Mommy and Daddy say that I should never go anywhere with a stranger."

"Yes, Claire, and you should always remember that. But Claire, you won't be alone. Your grandpa will be with us."

By now, the older fella had calmed down and seemed to understand that Michael was attempting to get them home safely. They got into Michael's truck and the girl said: "Mommy told me that when I am scared, I always have a guardian angel who is watching over me. Are you my guardian angel?"

"No, Claire, I'm not your guardian angel. But your guardian angel sent me to help you and grandpa get back home."

"Oh, so that's how my guardian angel works," said Claire.

"Where are you taking us?" asked Claire's grandpa. His voice registered more than a little anxiety.

"I'm going to try to get you home."

"OK; just don't try to pull any funny stuff."

Within two minutes Michael turned into the driveway of the farm he had passed moments earlier. It was the farm with the barn bearing the name "Duffy" painted in large white letters. As he proceeded down the driveway, a woman, who Michael assumed to be Mary Ann, Claire's mother, rushed out of the house.

As soon as the pickup stopped, Michael and Claire unfastened their seat belts and got out. Claire ran toward her mother, saying: "Mommy, Mommy."

"O, thank God you're safe. I've been looking all over for you. Where have you been?" Mary Ann asked, not really expecting an answer. The tone of her voice registered more relief than anger.

"I just wanted to go along with grandpa for a walk."

"How can I ever thank you, Mr...."

"Lattimore. I'm Michael Lattimore."

"I'm Mary Ann Robinson. Where did you find them?"

"Just a little ways down Q, heading toward 29."

"They got that far? I was just about to call the sheriff's department and ask them to search for them."

"Mommy, I remembered what you said about my guardian angel. This man said my guardian angel sent him to find us."

"Claire said that I must be her guardian angel, so I had to say something."

"Well, you did show up when they needed some help. And isn't that what guardian angels do?"

Mary Ann continued: "As you probably figured out, dad has dementia and along with it something called 'Sundowners Syndrome.' He's usually worse at night. That's when we really have to watch him. It's odd that he pulled something like this in the morning. Look at that, he's already dozing off in your truck – do you mind?"

"Of course not."

"With Sundowners, he's usually up most of the night, and that's when he's most apt to wander off. If he does head outdoors, he usually goes to the barn. He thinks he needs to milk the cows. There haven't been cows in the barn for almost fifteen years. That's when my husband and I felt we needed to sell them.

"Anyhow, last night was one of those difficult nights. I

think we only got about two hours of sleep. I assume that's why I fell asleep after I hung out the laundry. I came in and sat down on the sofa to rest a bit and must have dozed off. I remember dad was watching something on Animal Planet and Claire was in her room playing. They must have made their escape after I fell asleep. I must have been asleep for about an hour and when I woke up, the TV was still on, but dad wasn't in his recliner. I went to check on Clare and she wasn't in her room. Obviously, I panicked. I've been looking all over the place for them for the last ten or fifteen minutes. I was just getting my cell to call to sheriff's department when you pulled in."

"Thankfully, there's no need for that now. How long has your dad been dealing with dementia?" asked Michael.

"It's been just over a year. But he's only gotten bad since around Christmas."

"And I assume you haven't had a good night's sleep in weeks."

"No, neither I nor Lee, my husband."

"Have you thought about nursing care for your dad? A lot of nursing homes to offer special care for folks with various forms of dementia."

"Yes. We think about it. But then we feel guilty. This is his home. And he always said, 'If I ever have to go into one of those nursing homes, just shoot me.' Honestly, I'm not ready to take that step."

"Shooting, or the nursing home?" asked Michael – trying to lighten the moment.

"Obviously, the nursing home."

"Mary Ann, what about adult or senior daycare? Ever hear of that?"

"I thought day care was just for children. What's adult day care?"

"It's a place where seniors can go and spend the better part of the day. Often it includes a noon meal and a variety of activities," responded Michael.

"Do these places accommodate those with dementia?"

"I suppose it all depends on the place."

"I'm not from around here, but my guess is that Wausau would offer such a facility."

"I'll have to talk with Lee about this. After today, we've got to do something."

"I do know that adult day care is sometimes a good alliterative to full time residence in a nursing home. It won't get rid of the dementia. But it might give you a little break until you are ready to cross the bridge to some more extensive care."

"Thank you Michael for your suggestion. And thank you for finding them. I don't know if I could ever have forgiven myself had something happened to them."

"Well, it didn't. And I think the good Lord knows you are doing the best you can given your circumstances; so don't be too hard on yourself."

Mary Ann followed Michael back to his truck. She opened the passenger side door and gently awakened her father. "Dad, you're back home now. Go on into the house so Michael can be on his way."

Mr. Duffy crawled out of the truck, turned toward Michael, tipped his hat, and walked toward the house.

Claire, who had been playing on her swing set joined her grandpa, and, knowing that Michael was about to leave, blew her rescuer a kiss and waved good-bye.

Michael said good-bye to Mary Ann, and she responded: "Farewell, and thank you again."

Michael got in his pickup and returned to County Highway J.

Friday Noon

Michael continued on J until he met up with State Highway 153. He took it east until he came to US Highway 45. He turned right and headed straight for Clintonville. Michael intended to return to the back roads after he passed through Clintonville.

The donuts and juice that he had consumed at the Sky View just before checking out were long gone, and as he neared Clintonville, he thought: Since it's Friday and I'm in Wisconsin, there's bound to be a fish fry nearby. And I'm also in the heart of Supper Club country. Maybe one of these establishments will be open for lunch.

Supper Clubs were almost always family owned. They usually included a bar and were known for good food at reasonable prices.

It didn't take Michael very long to find a Supper Club on the edge of Clintonville. It had opened at 11:30. He stopped and entered. Immediately he noticed a sign indicating the special of the day. A perch plate for $14.50. Rather than occupying a table, Michael took a seat at the bar. He ordered a Baumeister Root Beer and a perch plate. He recalled that when he was a youth, a perch plate – consisting of an adequate amount of fried perch, and sides of french fries, coleslaw, and rye bread -- sold for a less than two dollars. He knew that sort of "deal" was long gone.

For centuries, Roman Catholics were prohibited from eating meat on Fridays. Thus, with an abundance of fresh fish from Lake Michigan and a high percentage of Wisconsin residents being Roman Catholic, the Friday fish fry became a staple. And even though the Friday "no meat" regulation is no longer in effect for Roman Catholics, the Friday fish fry tradition remains strong. Thankfully even though the supply of fresh fish from Lake Michigan -- especially lake perch -- has largely been depleted, suppliers have been able to secure a limited amount of perch from Lake Superior for their customers. So too, other varieties of fish including cod and haddock had become substitutes for lake perch in many places.

Michael enjoyed his meal and returned to his pickup. It was nearly 1:30 in the afternoon as he pulled out of the supper club and entered Clintonville.

Friday Early Afternoon

Michael drove through Clintonville on U.S. 51 and turned left onto County Highway I just south of town. He was heading east and was on his homestretch to Green Bay.

He had traveled only a few miles on County I when the sky suddenly clouded over. He looked in his rear-view mirror and he could see a bank of ominous black clouds in the west. The southern sky had also turned a steely gray. A storm-front was quickly approaching. Except for the rainstorm that had passed through Wausau the previous evening, Michael had enjoyed clear weather for his entire road trip.

Suddenly it was raining – "cats and dogs" as they say – pounding on his windshield and the pavement in front of him. After about five minutes the rain stopped, and the sunshine broke through the few remaining clouds. Michael decided to turn on the radio and check for a weather forecast.

And then it happened! He took his eyes off the road for only a second as he reached to turn on the radio, but when he returned his focus to the road, he saw a large dog immediately in front of him.

"A dog! No. A coyote!" Michael yelled as he braked and swerved to avoid the canine. He hit a patch of loose gravel and the rear end of his truck fishtailed. He lost control and a second later he veered off the right side of the road and into the ditch.

Michael tried backing out but went nowhere. The rain shower had wet the ground just enough to prevent Michael from gaining any traction. Michael tried again and again. He was able to go forward a few inches but could not back up the incline of the ditch. The more he accelerated the deeper he sunk into what was fast becoming a quagmire of mud. He hadn't realized that the rainstorm that hit Wausau the previous evening had evidently also soaked the area he was now traveling.

Michael tried "rocking it" – a maneuver of switching gears quickly between reverse and drive – back and forth, back and forth. It was technique that was often effective in snow, but it did not work in the muck.

I better get out and check for any damage, thought Michael. And then I suppose I'll have to call AAA Road Service. Certainty, not the way I expected to spend my afternoon.

Michael got out of the truck, bent down to view the undercarriage of his red pickup, and was pleased to notice no damage. As he pulled himself back up, he heard a sound he would always recognize: the putt putt putt of a John Deere tractor. The tractor was about two hundred yards behind him and moving toward Michael and his now stranded pickup.

A minute later the John Deere – pulling a chopper and wagon – arrived at Michael's location, and its driver -- wearing blue jeans and a red flannel shirt – got down from the seat.

"Looks like you're in kind of a fix," he said to Michael.

"Not something I was expecting. I swerved to miss what I thought was a dog. But it ended up being a coyote."

"I saw. I had just come out of the hay field back up the road and I saw you swerve. At least you didn't get hurt. And you didn't hit the coyote either."

"What's a coyote doing out in the middle of the day? I thought they only ran at night."

"I used to assume that, too. But in the last few years, I've seen one here and there right out in the broad sunlight."

"I guess you can add another coyote sighting to your list."

"By the way, I'm Angel Garcia. Most folks call me Ange – rhymes with range. I've been working for Mr. Clayton at the Sunnydale Farm for fifteen years – ever since I came to the states. That's Mr. Clayton's place," said Ange as he pointed to a farmstead located about a quarter mile down the road. "I'm just heading back after chopping the last of our hay crop."

"I'm Michael. Michael Lattimore. And I'm taking the back roads on my way home to Green Bay."

"How 'bout we get you out of there?"

"I don't want to be a bother; I've got AAA Road Service. I can call them, and they'll send out a wrecker to pull me out," replied Michael.

"Nah. Don't bother with that. I'll have you out in no time flat. This will be a piece of cake."

"Are you sure?" Michael asked.

"I wouldn't be telling you if I didn't want to do it. I'd have a hard time sleeping tonight if I didn't help you out. Mr. Clayton says to always keep a chain under my tractor seat. He says you never know when you need to use it."

"You mean like now?"

"Yeah; just give me a moment to unhook my chopper and wagon."

Angel went to the back of his tractor; disengaged the chopper and wagon; then he got on his tractor and pulled ahead a few feet. Once freed of the chopper and wagon, he backed his John Deere close to the rear bumper of Michael's truck. Then he got down from his tractor, reached under his seat and pulled out a heavy-duty chain, hooking one end to a large hole in a metal plate at the back of his John Deere and the other end to the frame of Michael's truck.

Ange returned to Michael and said: "You get in your truck; and put it in neutral. I'll pull forward slowly until the chain is tight. Once it's tight, I'll ease forward some more. I should be able to pull you out in no time. When you feel your front wheels are on the shoulder of the road, hit the brakes. I don't want you to end up banging your nice truck into the back of my tractor."

"Got it," said Michael.

Michael got in his truck and put it in neutral while Ange climbed up on the seat of the tractor.

Just like he indicated, Ange pulled forward just a bit, picking up any slack in the chain. Then he slowly crept forward as Michael felt his truck ascending the incline. Less than a minute later, Michael's Ford truck was back on the road. Ange jumped down from the tractor and unhooked both ends of the chain. Then as Michael pulled forward and to the safely of road's shoulder, Ange returned his chain to its place under his seat and maneuvered his tractor to the other side of the road. The two fellas then met in the center of the road.

"Just like I told you – a piece of cake," said Ange.

"How much do I owe you?" asked Michael.

"You're kidding; that's just what we do around here. We help folks out."

"Well, I really appreciate the help. I must say, you sure live up to your name."

"How's that?"

"You're like an angel. Like a guardian angel you arrived when I needed help and you helped me without hesitation."

"Maybe I should tell you that when I was born, my papa wanted to call me Pedro. But my mother said, 'No.' She said I looked like such a little angel. She won the argument, and so I'm Angel. But like I said, most folks around here call me Ange."

"Ange, how long have you been working for Mr. Clayton?"

"I've been with him for just over fifteen years. When I first came here I missed my family and my little village. I was so happy when Rita and our two young children could join me. It took a little while, but we have now found a home here thanks to Mr. and Mrs. Jamison. I'd like to think we've put down some roots."

"I thought you said you worked for Mr. Clayton."

"Clayton is his first name. His last name is Jamison; But I've always called him Mr. Clayton.".

Ange noticed a Packers decal on the back window of Michael's truck cab. "How do you think our Packers will do this year?" Ange asked. "I played soccer when I was younger, but I've come to like American football. Couldn't help it with all the Packers fans around here."

"You should live in Green Bay. It's like a religion and Lambeau Field is the cathedral. As far as how they'll do this year, your guess is as good as mine."

"I've been on the waiting list for season tickets for eight years now. I don't know how many thousand are still ahead of me," reported Ange.

"Our daughter Sarah is on the waiting list too. A couple of years ago she said: 'I'll probably get tickets when I'm a hundred. They'll wheel me in, and I'll watch the game and then I'll die."'

"At least she has a sense of humor about it."

"Well, I better be on my way. Thank you again, Ange."

"Michael, I've got an idea. Why don't you follow me back to the farm? I see you got yourself a little muddy. I suppose that happened when you were looking under your pickup. I saw that you were checking for damage. You can clean yourself up a bit. Anyhow, Mr. Clayton and I usually take a break in the mid-afternoon. I'd like you to meet him," said Ange.

"I don't want to put you out."

"Like I said before, I wouldn't have asked if I didn't mean it."

"OK. I'll follow you."

Angel backed up his tractor, reattached his chopper and wagon, and proceeded down the road. Michael followed at a safe distance.

Friday Mid Afternoon

As Michael pulled into the driveway he scanned the surroundings. He eyed a well-kept barn, several outbuildings including one which Michael assumed was a machine shed, and two residences. One was a stately two-story brick home that Michael guessed was eighty or ninety years old and which Michael thought was the Jamison residence; and the other a small frame house that Michael assumed was Ange's place. He had seen several similar farm layouts in his travels.

Michael followed Ange to the machine shed. Standing at its entrance was Mr. Jamison. He was accompanied by a rather lively dog. Michael couldn't identify the breed; but it looked like a cross between a collie and a German shepherd.

"Mr. Clayton, I want you to meet Michael. He's from Green Bay. We met on the road," announced Ange.

"How do you do, Michael? You can call me Clay. Ange has been working for me for over fifteen years and he still calls me Mr. Clayton. I told him to call me Clay, but he can't seem to break the habit."

"Nice to meet you, Clay. Before we go any further I need to tell you what Ange just did for me. I swerved to avoid a coyote, hit some gravel, and ended up in the ditch. While I was inspecting my truck for any damage, Ange came along with the John Deere pulling the chopper and wagon, and without any hesitation, he pulled me out. What a lifesaver. I didn't have to wait for AAA Road Service to come and pull me out," reported a grateful Michael.

"Did Ange happen to tell you that I always remind him to keep a good chain under the seat of the tractor? You never know when you'll need it" said Clay.

"He sure did. That was one of the first things he told me when he arrived on the scene."

"That sounds like Ange. He's the best hired hand we've ever had. My wife Nadine and I were not able to have children – that presents difficulties when you farm – so we've had a series of hired hands. Never needed another after we hired Ange. He's been a good and faithful employee and I'm glad he has stayed with us as long as he has."

"Yes, Mr. Clayton, you've been good to us, too. You and Nadine helped to bring my Rita and our children here, and you've always paid me a fair wage," said Ange.

"And watching Miguel and Maria grow up – knowing we could never have children of our own -- it's the closest thing we had to having our own children. That's been a real joy and a blessing we didn't expect."

"Mr. Clayton, I told Michael he could stop here and get himself cleaned up a bit. I'll take him over to our place."

"No need to go over there. Let's go inside the home place and get some iced tea. We can continue our conversation in the kitchen," Clay offered. "Michael can use the bathroom while I fetch the iced tea. And I can probably find some sugar cookies. Nadine made a batch last night after supper."

As the three walked toward the house, Clay leaned over to Michael and said: "So you say Ange rescued you. Wait until we get inside and sit down and I'll tell you the story of how he rescued me. I really owe my life to him."

They entered the house and Clayton pointed Michael in the direction of the bathroom. "There should be a towel hanging up on the rack just to the left of the shower; go ahead and use it," instructed Clay.

After Michael returned from the bathroom, he and Ange took seats at the large kitchen table. Meanwhile, as Clayton approached the refrigerator Michael noticed two series of school pictures running vertically on the refrigerator door. One showed a boy with dark hair and the other was girl with hairstyles that seemed to change from year to year. The boy was a spittin' image of Ange.

"Miguel and Maria, I assume?" Michael commented.

"Yeah, school pictures from elementary school all the way through their first years of high school. They sure grow up fast," Ange replied proudly.

Clay brought out a large pitcher of iced tea from the refrigerator and reached for a plate of cookies that were on the counter. He placed the tea and cookies on the table.

"Sorry it's not a nice cold beer; but we just don't keep

beer in the house anymore."

"Iced tea is fine, Clay," Michael responded.

They each poured a glass and took a good gulp.

Turning to Michael, Clay said: "Speaking of beer, reminds me of what I was mentioning to you on the way in – how Angel rescued me."

"Well, go on – I'm all ears."

"Remember back in '88 we had that drought."

"Yes, we were living in Ohio then, but I know Wisconsin got hit hard."

"You wouldn't believe it; relentless heat, no rain for weeks; crops dying in the fields. Fortunately, some folks down south knew about our circumstances, and they sent caravans of hay up our way. Maybe they were just returning the favor, because the previous year, the southeastern states had experienced a similar drought and we Wisconsin farmers sent truckloads of hay down to them. Their assistance helped some of us get through the rough time. Thankfully, Nadine had just finished her training to be a dental hygienist and got a part-time job with Dr. Story and his partner, Dr. Schubert in Clintonville. By the way, she's still with them after all these years – full time now.

"But even with Nadine working, and the hay were received, I still worried if we would be able to keep our heads above water. Well, to forget about my worries, I started drinking. No. I should say, I changed my way of drinking. Sure, I used to have a beer once in a great while, but I started drinking – heavy. Often a six pack or more a day. And then I discovered brandy. I always heard Wisconsin was known for its brandy consumption; and I decided that I wanted to find out what was so special about it. I guess I thought it was special, because I started drinking it – a lot of it. But really, I just wanted something to numb my worries about the drought and the possibilities of not only losing my crops but losing the farm.

"But then Nadine's mom died and left us nearly three hundred thousand dollars."

"So your financial worries were over?" asked Michael.

"Yes, I worried less about finances; but I didn't quit my drinking. I didn't think I had a problem.

"After all, I thought alcoholics are those guys begging on the street corner or stumbling out of some bar. I was still handling my farm work, milking, planting, and harvesting my crops, and with the help of Fred – our previous hired hand – the work was getting done and the bills were being paid."

All the while Clay was speaking, Ange listened closely – even though had heard the story many times before.

"One day I went to the jar on the counter," Clay continued as he pointed to a large ceramic cookie jar. "It's where we always keep some cash. I reached in for a twenty. I was going to go over to Sneed's Market to get a bottle of brandy, but the money jar was empty. I accused Fred of robbing us. Only thing is, he didn't. I had forgotten that I had taken the money two days earlier and used it to buy you know what. Well, after my false accusation, Fred up and quit – and probably rightfully so. He had had enough of my shenanigans. But that still didn't stop me from my drinking. By then I had been at it for too many years; and I was hooked.

"I got to tell you, I don't know how or why Nadine stayed with me through it all. Obviously, she's always taken the 'for better or worse' part of our wedding vows seriously. But I know she kept hoping I would come to my senses.

"After Fred left we tried getting along without a hired hand for a while, but I just couldn't handle it. So we put a help wanted ad in the paper for a hired hand. Ange responded and we hired him.

"I could tell Ange didn't appreciate my drinking, especially when I'd holler at him for no good reason. And I know he thought I'd do something stupid like roll the tractor over on myself or get too close to the power take-off. Thank God, those things didn't happen.

"Then Ange -- well, he and Nadine -- cooked up a plan.

"One hot summer night, Nadine and I heard a knock on the door at about 10 o'clock. I answered the door, and it was Ange. He stumbled in and plopped on the sofa. 'Have you been drinking?' I asked him."

Clay momentarily suspended his story as he turned from Michael and looked toward Ange and asked: "And what did you say, Ange?"

"No more than you."

"That's right," he said, "No more than you."

"And so I hollered back to Ange, 'You have no right speaking to me like that?'

"'Well then,'" Ange countered, 'What gives you the right to speak to Nadine and me that way you do when you've been drinking? And no, I haven't been drinking. I'm just trying to show you what it's like when you are drinking.'

Then Ange said something that stopped me in my tracks. He told me what Miguel had said to him one night as he was about to say his bedtime prayers: "I like Mr. Clayton and Ms. Nadine, but when Mr. Clayton starts yelling, I'm get afraid of him."

"That did it. Suddenly, it was like I was looking in a mirror; and I didn't like what I was seeing. I didn't want to be that man in the mirror. I didn't want little Miguel to be afraid of me. There's no way I wanted to do anything that would upset those precious little ones – Miguel and Maria. But obviously I did. And that was over a dozen years ago, and I haven't had a drop since. That's why I said, 'Angel rescued me.'

"It was an intervention and had they not done it, who knows what kind of shape I'd be in today; or if I'd even still be alive."

"What a powerful story," said Michael.

"I should tell you, I started going to AA right after that

night. Went through the Twelve Step program. And I've been blessed to be a sponsor to three other guys over the years. And yes, I continue to go to a weekly meeting. I admit I am an alcoholic; but I like to think I'm a recovering alcoholic – thanks to Ange and my dear Nadine."

"Thank you for being so candid," replied Michael.

"Well, enough of me. What brings you over this way from Green Bay?"

"I'm from Green Bay, but I've been on the road for ten days. So I'm now on the home stretch. I've been traveling around the state – to most of the dairy farm regions. And I've been talking with a lot of rural folks –mostly dairy farmers like you -- and asking them about all the changes they've been facing the last several years, and how they're being affected by all the changes."

"What makes you want to undertake such a project?" asked both Clay and Ange simultaneously.

"Well, I grew up in the country – Manitowoc County. Not on a farm but surrounded by dairy farms. After I graduated from college I lived in Ohio for several years, but when I came back to Wisconsin I was shocked by all the changes I saw on the rural landscape.

"I'm a middle school social studies teacher and I was able to secure a grant from a foundation to do this on the field research."

"What have you been finding out?" asked Clay.

"Probably things you are already familiar with: stagnant milk prices, less children either available or willing to take over the farm when mom and dad want to retire, competition from the huge farms, and the high cost of equipment. Then there's more and more farmers selling their herds; and certainly, a lot fewer 'family-size farms' -- those that milk fifty to eighty cows."

Clay rubbed his forehead and said: "I can add one more change or challenge to your list: It's a change over the past thirty years or so that is causing a problem: America's shifting taste preferences are leading to a decline in fluid milk consumption. Not only soda, but energy drinks and even soy milk. And I'd swear that every time I go to the grocery store, they're promoting some new kind of flavored water. Who knows what's next? And here's the 'catch 22:' Milk production per cow continues to rise – you'd think that would be a good thing. So farmers are capable of producing more milk which results in more supply at a time when demand is declining. And then there's our exports. You never know when a country to which we've been exporting dairy products will slap a tariff on their imports. Again, the result is that the demand goes down."

"Do you ever think about getting out of it – selling your herd and moving to town and renting your crop land?" asked Michael.

"I think every one of us dairy farmers thinks about that. And in the last twenty years I know that over half of my farmer friends have sold their herds. And yes, most have kept their crop land and rent it to the big guys who need the crops. Truth is: There's pretty good money to be made in renting your good crop land.

"But I haven't answered your question. Yes, I considered selling out, but then I think: What would I do? I've been farming all my life. Farming isn't just a job for me. It's who I am. I'd miss my cattle, the planting and harvesting, and even all the smells that go along with dairy farming."

"You certainly aren't alone. Those exact same feelings have been expressed by several of the folks I've had the privilege of meeting over the past ten days," offered Michael.

Then Michael continued: "I assume you'll need to get ready for milking and I need to be on my way. Thank you for your hospitality, and thank you again, Ange, for coming to my rescue."

"Just glad to be at the right place at the right time."

Michael got up and as he approached the door, he turned and said, "So long, Clay and Ange."

"Goodbye, Michael; if you ever get over this way again, stop in," said Clay.

"I'll be sure to do that."

"Blessings to you, my friend," said Ange.

"And to you, Ange."

Michael stepped outside and as he approached his truck he thought: Yes, I've met several friends over the past week and a half. And what a blessing that has been.

Friday Late Afternoon

Before pulling out of the Jamison's driveway, Michael checked for oncoming traffic. As he looked west he saw that the sky was again starting to cloud over. Seeing no oncoming vehicles from either direction, he turned east onto County Highway I. "I wonder if we're in for more rain?" he asked himself. "I'll find out what the weather forecaster has to say about this?"

Evidently, Michael had not tuned in to any station when he had turned his radio on just before his mishap with the coyote. He quickly found a clear channel. The broadcast was from a Christian radio station in Suring, a small town about an hour north of Michael's present location. The well-loved hymn "Amazing Grace" was being played.

Even though Michael had both heard and sung "Amazing Grace" countless times, the song's third verse seemed to speak to him in a new way: "Through many dangers, toils, and snares I have already come; 'tis grace has brought me safe thus far, and grace will lead me home."

"And grace will lead me home." As the words continued to resound in Michael's mind, he considered his ten days of travel and announced: "Yes, 'grace has brought me safe thus far, and grace will lead me home,' but grace has also 'meet me on my way home.' For that's certainly been my experience today with Ange arriving out of nowhere and coming to my rescue. It was an unexpected and undeserved gift. It was grace."

Michael's contemplative spirit continued. He began to wonder if there was a direct relationship between "grace" and "home." That consideration transported him back to the first day of his sabbatical travel. He had only driven a little over an hour when he made his first stop. It was at his undergraduate college in rural Sheboygan County. He had pulled off County Highway M and entered the campus of Lakeland University.

Upon his arrival he had felt as if he had come home. But this wasn't the only time he had experienced this feeling of "coming home." Since he moved back to Wisconsin, he had been to the college on several occasions. And it was always the same. He always felt like he had come home.

Walking on the Lakeland campus on his first day of sabbatical travel he then remembered a phrase from the school's "Alma Mater." It was a phrase that sought to describe the experience of those who had ever been affiliated with the college – a phrase that was meant to describe the school: "No matter where I roam a place that's always home." Michael concurred: I have certainly found these lyrics to be absolutely true. For no matter where I've roamed, this place is always home.

Approaching the university's chapel that had been constructed the year following his graduation, Michael gazed at the large cross that rose alongside the building, and he questioned: But what is it that makes this place feel like home -- not only for me, but for so many others?

Michael sat down on the steps leading to the chapel and dug deeper into his memory bank. He thought back to the day he arrived on the Lakeland campus as a seventeen-year-old. The only person he knew on the entire campus was the Admissions Director; and he had only spent an hour or so with him the previous winter. Michael recalled how he soon discovered friends and a staff that truly cared. Not only was the faculty helpful, but everyone from the housekeeping and maintenance staff to the administration always took time for any student's concerns. And not only did he find the school to be a place of intellectual, emotional, and spiritual growth and thus a place of self-discovery, he sensed something more –

Looking up at the cross looming above him, he said out loud: "This is a place where I was accepted. And I was accepted not because of anything I did but accepted just because I had enrolled and was a now a part of the campus community. And I began to realize that this place – for me – was a place of grace. That's what makes Lakeland feel like 'home' to me. It's grace." And then he thought: Here grace wasn't only a theological concept, but it was a living reality. All I had to do was open my heart and receive it.

After his revelation Michael stood up and started to walk back to his pickup. As he continued to look around the campus he took in several of the changes that had occurred since his time as a student. He found himself thinking: I hope that spirit of grace will continue to pervade the university so that it will be a home to all who are now, or ever will be, a part of the Lakeland community.

A couple of rain drops began to pelt Michael's windshield and his mind returned to the present. And suddenly, he had the answer to his original question regarding a relationship between grace and home: Yes, there is a relationship. Grace not only "leads us home;" grace makes a place home.

After Michael concluded his reminiscing, he decided to give Elaine a call and let her know when he hoped to arrive home. Although she was teaching remedial reading for the Green Bay School district, it was late afternoon, and he knew she would be home. He turned the volume down on his radio and hit his speed dial. When Elaine answered, Micheal replied: "Hello, Grace... I mean Elaine."

"What did you call me?"

"I guess I called you Grace," admitted Michael

Not wanting to let Michael "off the hook" easily, Elaine teased: "Did you pick up another woman on the way?"

"Of course not. I've been thinking about grace – not a woman named Grace, but about the term grace as it is found in the Bible."

"I should have known. You always say it's your favorite word from the Bible."

"It is."

"What's up? You sound a little shook up. Is everything alright?

"Everything's fine now."

"What do you mean, now? What happened?"

"I had to get pulled out of the ditch."

"Are you hurt?"

"No. Just my pride. I'm fine. A coyote ran in front of me and as I tried to avoid hitting it, I ran into some loose gravel and slid into the ditch. Thankfully, no damage to the truck or me. Well, the truck's a muddy mess. I spun the wheels and flung mud all over the place while trying to get out."

"So you got out somehow?"

"Yes, thanks to Angel."

"What angel?"

"Angel. A fella named Angel – folks call him 'Ange;' but he was like my guardian angel. He pulled me out with his John Deere. He was on the road behind me and saw it happen."

"I'm glad you didn't get hurt. You're fortunate that someone was there for you. I know you've been traveling those back roads that don't get much traffic." Elaine paused and then continued: "No wonder your mind is on grace. Sounds like you've been graced by an Angel... I'm ready for you to be home."

"I am too. I should tell you where I am. I'm east of

Clintonville and I hope to be home in a about an hour."

"I'll be waiting. I'm glad you're finishing up sooner than you originally thought."

"Me too, Sweetheart."

"I'll see you soon."

Michael turned up the volume on his radio just in time to catch the weather report: Highs in the mid 70's with intermittent showers until 8 P.M..

Sure enough; about ten minutes after talking with Elaine, the rain showers intensified. But again it lasted only a few minutes. Maybe it's washed some of the mud off, Michael hoped.

As he continued eastward, Michael noticed a faint rainbow ahead of him on the horizon. Michael imagined the rainbow to be over Green Bay. He thought: There's supposed to be a pot of gold at the end of a rainbow. There's something better at the end of this rainbow: Elaine.

Michael continued toward Green Bay. He had "stair-stepped" his way south and east and was now traveling on State Highway 54. He knew he was getting close to the city when he saw a large dark green structure looming in the distance. It was Lambeau Field – home of the Green Bay Packers. He recalled the first Packers game he had attended. It was in Milwaukee at a place called County Stadium. For a number of years, the Packers played "home" games at both Green Bay and Milwaukee. However, some years ago the Packers began playing all their home games in Green Bay at Lambeau Field. He remembered that the facility was not called Lambeau Field until the mid-1960's. When it first opened in 1957 it was called the New City Stadium to distinguish it from the older City Stadium located on the opposite side of town. The name was changed from City Stadium to Lambeau Field shortly after the death of Curly Lambeau, an early player and coach who was also instrumental in the team's founding over one hundred years ago.

Twenty minutes later he pulled into the driveway at 3346 Bay Cliff Drive. He was home. Elaine rushed out of the house and greeted him with a big hug and kiss. She led him into the house to the dining room where the table was adorned with two candles waiting to be lit and set with the china they seldom used.

Handing Michael a lighter, Elaine asked Michael: "Will you do the honors?" Michael obliged and lit the candles. Then Elaine said: "Excuse me for a moment." She returned with a platter filled with fish – fresh broiled whitefish caught by Door County fishers, and fried perch from Lake Superior. Elaine preferred the whitefish and Michael the perch. Returning from the kitchen a second time, she presented a second platter. This one was filled with french fries. Her third trip to the kitchen resulted in a bowl of coleslaw and some fresh rye bread.

Michael didn't have the heart to tell Elaine he had eaten fish for the past two meals. Anyhow, the fish sandwich he had eaten last night was cod; and the fish fry he had for lunch was not nearly as tasty as Elaine's.

"Eat up," said Elaine. "If we hurry up, well still have time to go over to Kohl's and look for baby clothes."

"I was thinking, Elaine, since we don't know if the baby is a boy or a girl, we can't buy blue or pink; so maybe we should look for one of those one-piece things in either green or gold; like maybe a little Packers outfit."

"I think what you are referring to is called a 'onesie,' Dear," said Elaine. "So you're hoping our first grandchild will be a Packers fan."

Life doesn't get any better than this, Michael thought to himself as he looked out of the dining room window to his well-traveled pickup. Then he turned to Elaine and, picking up their conversation of an hour earlier, said: "Grace has not only led me home, but grace has also met me here."

Epilogue – An Update on the Characters from the Five Volumes

Two summers after Michael's sabbatical journey, he decided to retrace his tracks. This time Elaine was able to accompany him. Michael was eager to introduce Elaine to those he had met and to see how they were faring.

Their first stop was to the Erickson farm outside of Darlington. Joe and Linda Erickson continued to live on their home farm that has been in the Erickson family for several generations. Their grief resulting from the deaths of their daughter, son in law and young granddaughter that had largely enveloped their lives two years earlier had significantly subsided – not completely, but significantly.

They learned that Sam, their hired hand who had been with them for over twenty years, was beginning to purchase the dairy herd. And, if Joe and Linda decided to move off the farm, Sam would be given the first opportunity to buy the Erickson acreage, house, barn, and outbuildings.

After visiting the Erickson's, they drove to Platteville where they checked into the Hillview Lodge. When they went for supper at Jim's Diner, Betty, who was standing behind the counter, recognized Michael and unashamedly spoke: "Long time no see. Come here and let me give you a hug." After supper Michael and Elaine returned to the Hillview and Michael called Jack

Tollefson. Jack immediately invited Michael and Elaine to a cookout at his farm for the following day. Jack said he and Mary would invite Jake and his family to join them.

And so, the next day after the outdoor meal of brats, burgers, potato salad, beans, lemonade, and ice cream, they all put their lawn chairs in a circle and carried on a conversation. Michael and Elaine learned that Jack and Mary's son, Andy, returned from Great Britain and was now employed as a research analyst with the State Department of Agriculture. Angie was pleased to tell Michael and Elaine that she had graduated in June, and following in her cousins' footsteps, was ready to begin studies at Ripon College.

Jake and Kathy Tollefson continued to operate the farm adjacent to Jack and Mary. John, their older son, remains in the Air Force and is considering making it a career. James, their younger son, finished the "farm short course" offered by the University of Wisconsin and hopes to take over the family farm when his folks retire. Darlene, their daughter, had successfully defended her doctoral thesis in the spring and had been awarded her Ph. D. from Vanderbilt University. The previous summer she married Craig who had graduated from Vanderbilt's medical school. He was now in residency at the regional medical center in Marquette, Michigan. Darlene is serving as a pastor in a small town outside Marquette. They just adopted a black Labrador they have appropriately named "Vandy" in recognition of their graduate and medical schools.

Jack and Mary told Michael and Elaine that Ed Duncan continues to operate the Chevy dealership and was recently honored by General Motors for outstanding service to customers for thirty years.

Jake said that Pete Samuelson made the decision to transform his feed mill into "Pete's Treats." Jake further reported that Pete specializes in all sorts and candy, ice cream, soda, and sports drinks; that he's open eight months of the year and receives a steady supply of customers from the nearby recreational trail. Jake went on to say, "And yes, before you ask, two of his regular customers are Cliff Engelbretsen and me. And speaking of Cliff, he just proposed to Judy Waller, a woman who had taught high school English for thirty-five years. I believe you met her at Jerry and Nita's barn dance when they celebrated their 50th anniversary. Well, Jerry and Nita just celebrated their 52nd wedding anniversary with another barn dance. This one occurred with no incidents."

Then Kathy said that Pastor Ann remains the minister at St. John's Church. She officiated at the wedding of Darlene and Craig and will also preside at the wedding of Cliff and Judy. James, sitting to the right of his mother, smiled upon hearing Pastor Ann's name. He still had a secret crush on his pastor.

After the good visit with the Tollefsons, Michael and Elaine made their way to Lacrosse and checked in at the Riverview Motel. As Tom Snyder, the proprietor, was getting a room key for Michael and Elaine, he turned to Michael and asked: "You've stayed here before, haven't you?" Michael re-introduced himself and asked if Bill and Carol were still running the bar and restaurant next door. Tom indicated they were. So after putting their luggage in their room, Michael and

Elaine walked over to the establishment which had been renamed the Riverview Supper Club. Michael thought that changing the name from Riverview Bar and Grill to Riverview Supper Club was a good idea, since supper clubs throughout Wisconsin have a reputation for good food in a relaxed atmosphere. And the Riverview certainly offered that.

As soon as Michael and Elaine entered, Bill, standing behind the bar, spoke out: "Well, look what the cat dragged in." He called to Carol who was in the kitchen: "Come and see who's here." Then he offered Michael and Elaine "Old Fashioneds" – on the house. The Lattimore's visit with Bill and Carol was as good as the ribeyes Carol prepared for them.

After checking out the next morning, Michael and Elaine started toward Colby. Before they reached Abottsford, they arrived at the location of the barn fire that Michael had come upon two years earlier. Michael was glad to see that a new metal structure now stood at the location where he had seen smoldering remains two years ago. About twenty head of Holstein heifers grazed in a nearby field.

Michael and Elaine stopped for gas and a break at the convenience store on the edge of Neillsville. As he checked out, Michael asked the clerk at the counter if she knew whether Herm – whose name Michael had overheard when he stopped at the same convenience store on his sabbatical -- was still milking after the fire of two summers ago.

"I can't answer that, but I'm sure my manager can." And with that she approached an open door behind the counter and said, "Hey Hank, there's a fella here who's got a question you can probably answer."

Hank walked through the door, approached the counter, and asked Michael: "How might I help you?"

Michael responded: "Two years ago I was traveling up 13 and a couple of miles back I noticed the aftermath of a barn fire. When I stopped for gas here, someone said the barn belonged to a fella named Herm. I'm just wondering: Is he's milking again?"

"Yeah, he sure is. When he rebuilt, he just constructed a heifer shed. His milk cows are still at Gregg Little's place. Gregg had taken them after the fire; and he and Herm worked out a deal. Gregg said: 'I've got this practically new milking parlor and no cows of my own. It doesn't do anybody any good not being used.' And so I heard that Herm is buying the milking barn and renting some of the surrounding pastureland."

"Sounds like it has worked out pretty good for the two of them," said Michael.

Passing through Neillsville, Michael turned to Elaine and said: "I remember this location. This is where I was when you called me to tell me that Simon and Ali were expecting little John Michael, although at the time we had no idea whether it was a boy or a girl."

Just before they arrived in Colby, they approached the farm of Sid and Janice Roberson. Michael questioned whether they should stop, but Elaine said: "Why don't we stop? I know you've been wondering how they're doing?"

As they pulled into Sid and Janice's driveway, they noticed that Janice was hanging out the laundry. She heard Michael's truck and turned. Immediately she recognized Michael as he stepped from the pickup. She approached Michael and said: "My, my – what a pleasant surprise. Let me run in the barn and get Sid. He's in the barn doing something with the calves we're raising."

Janice returned in a moment and a few seconds later Sid hustled out of the barn. Immediately, Michael introduced Elaine to Sid and Janice.

Michael and Elaine learned that the Roberson's were doing well. They had participated in a farmers' support group in Wausau for the past two years and were about to begin a similar support group in Colby. And after having to sell his milking herd two years earlier, Sid continued to grow corn and beans and has been raising calves for a couple of nearby farms. He often visits his good friend and neighbor, Alfred. And when at Alfred's place he gets to see "Daisy May." She had been Sid's favorite milk cow and Alfred had rescued her on the day that Sid's herd was auctioned.

Michael and Elaine spent the night in Abbotsford. The next morning – after sleeping in to almost check out time – they started out for Wausau. On the way they passed St. Stansilaus Church, rectory, and cemetery. Michael slowed so that had could gaze into the cemetery. He was hoping that Helen and Junior were making their regular visit to Boyd and John's graves. He saw no one so he continued.

Soon they approached the Roadside Cafe and Michael

asked Elaine: "Are you ready for some lunch?"

"If you are," Elaine responded.

So they stopped. As soon as they opened the door, Michael looked in the direction of the table toward the rear of the dining room where he had been with Junior and Helen and their friends Clyde and Dorothea two years earlier. The table was vacant. But then Michael heard familiar voices coming from the other side of the dining room. As he turned, he saw those he was hoping to see. There sat Junior and Helen, Clyde and Dorothea. Another woman, whose back was turned to the door, accompanied them.

When Helen looked up, she immediately recognized Michael. She squealed with excitement. Junior, Clyde and Dorothea followed Helen's eyes toward the door. They all immediately motioned for Michael and Elaine to join them. After Michael introduced Elaine to the group, Michael and Elaine learned that Helen and Junior continue their monthly visits to the graves of Boyd and John. And the woman sitting among them? It was Clyde and Dorothea's daughter, Christine, who had been widowed and recently moved back home from Oregon. Growing up as neighbors, she and Junior had been friends in their younger years. They were now "seeing each other."

As Michael and Elaine approached Wausau they stopped at the bank in Marathon where George Sullivan continued to serve as a loan officer. George was pleased to announce that their son Tanner had entered the 4-H oratorical contest the year after Michael had first met him and had been awarded first place at the Wisconsin Valley Fair. Then he finished third in the state contest. Tanner was on his way to the University of Wisconsin in Madison in the fall. "As a member of the National Honor Society, Tanner was the recipient of a couple of sizable scholarships," reported his proud father.

After spending the night at the Sky View Inn, Michael took Elaine up Rib Mountain. She relished the view and said it reminded her of the trips she and her family took to the mountains of Pennsylvania during her childhood.

Soon they were traveling east toward Green Bay. They passed the Duffy farm and saw Claire playing in the yard and her mother, Mary Ann, puttering in a flower bed. Mary Ann's father, Duffy, was nowhere in sight. They decided to stop, but only for a minute. Mary Ann welcomed them and said that her dad was a regular at the Morningside Adult Daycare Center in Wausau. She said that a van from the Center comes and picks him up at 8 o'clock Monday through Friday and that her dad seems to be enjoying himself at the Center.

Soon Michael and Elaine were at the location where Micheal had slid off the road in his effort to dodge the coyote. And a moment later they were in front of the Jamison farm. "Let's see if anyone is home," said Michael. Elaine knew how grateful Michael was for the help Ange had given Michael two years earlier.

As they pulled in, Clay stepped out from behind a hay wagon and gazed at the pickup entering his driveway. He recognized Michael and motioned for him to pull up next to the picnic table. When Michael and Elaine got out of the truck, Clay warmly shook Michael's hand as Michael introduced Elaine. No sooner had Elaine informed Clay – "We've been following the path Michael took two years ago on his sabbatical journey, and it sure has been wonderful meeting many of the folks he met along the way" -- that the familiar putt putt putt of a John Deere tractor was heard. Soon Ange pulled in. He saw Michael, stopped the tractor, jumped off and warmly greeted Michael. As Michael introduced Elaine to Ange, Clay went into the house and in a moment came back out carrying a large tray holding a pitcher of lemonade, four ice-filled glasses, a plate of chocolate chip cookies and a wad of napkins.

Ange had good news: "Miguel just finished his first year of college," he said with a proud smile on his face. "He's at Lakeland."

"You've got to be kidding me! Lakeland?" replied a surprised Michael.

"Yes, Lakeland. It's not too far away. Only about an hour's drive to the campus."

"Ange, I'm really very pleased to hear that. Because that's where I went for my undergraduate education. I hope he enjoys the place as much as I did."

"I think he's having a good time. He has gotten good grades and was on the cross country and track teams. He even calls it 'his second home.' We checked out a number of schools including two or three in the University of Wisconsin system. But then someone in church said that one of Lakeland's priorities is to attract those who are first generation college students.

Since Miguel is in that category, we decided to check it out. And with the financial aid they offered, the costs are comparable to the state schools. Plus, when we were on campus, everyone made us feel so welcome."

"I'm glad to hear that. That welcoming spirit was something I appreciated years ago during my student days. I guess it's woven deep into the college's character. I guess I should say 'University's character,' since it changed from being a college to a university not too many years ago. I was afraid they might have lost that spirit when they went from a 'college' to a 'university.' Evidently, it remains."

Ange went on: "We'd thought Miguel would still need to get a loan for some other costs like books and some other fees, but one night while Rita and I were filling out a form for additional financial aid, Mr. Clayton knocked on our door and without saying a word he handed us a check for $5,000. Then he spoke, saying: 'I hope this helps.'

"We wanted to refuse the money, but Mr. Clayton insisted, saying: 'This is our gift of gratitude. Ange, you saved me from my self-destruction, and I am grateful.'"

Then Clay added to Ange's story: "I told Ange, 'As soon as you helped me to quit my drinking, I began to put aside the money I would have spent on beer and brandy.' Nadine and I thought, since we couldn't have children of our own, why can't we help out with Rita and Ange's kids?

"We actually put in about $30 each week into a special

account, and it has grown rather nicely over the years. It's no secret now, but we plan on doing the same for Maria when she graduates from high school."

After visiting a brief while longer and knowing that Ange and Mr. Jamison had chores to attend to, Michael and Elaine got back on the road. An hour and a half later, Michael and Elaine were pulling into their driveway on Bay Cliff Drive.

A Word on Michael and Elaine and their family:

Michael and Elaine's son, Simon and his spouse, Ali, are proud parents of John Michael, now an active 16-month-old. Simon continues to teach 3rd grade and Ali is now the branch manager at a credit union in Ripon.

Sarah still lives in Milwaukee and is an assistant to the mayor. She advises the mayor on issues related to housing and job development.

Elaine continues to teach early elementary students in the Green Bay School district. Her greatest joy comes whenever she helps a student discover a love for reading.

Michael remains a middle school social studies teacher at Fairview School in Green Bay. Nominated by a group of students and parents, he has just been named the district's "Teacher of the Year."

www.ingramcontent.com/pod-product-compliance
Lightning Source LLC
Chambersburg PA
CBHW071408070526
44578CB00002B/523